DATE DUE

AUG 0 9 2008			

ALSO BY HELEN PALMER

*The Enneagram: Understanding Yourself
and the Others in Your Life*

*The Enneagram in Love & Work: Understanding
Your Intimate & Business Relationships*

The Pocket Enneagram

UNDERSTANDING THE 9 TYPES OF PEOPLE

Helen Palmer

HarperSanFrancisco
An Imprint of HarperCollins*Publishers*

To the next generation—the children of our students

Library of Congress Cataloging-in-Publication Data
Palmer, Helen.
The pocket enneagram : understanding the 9 types of people / Helen Palmer. — 1st ed.
p.   cm.
ISBN 0–06–251327–3 (pbk.)
1. Enneagram.   2. Typology (Psychology)   I. Title.
BF698.3.E54P36 1995   95–4044
155.2'6—dc20   CIP

99 ❖ HAD 10 9 8 7 6

Contents

Nine Points of View

The personality types described in this book are part of a human development system called the Enneagram. *Ennea* means "nine" in Greek, and *gram* means "model"—the diagram models nine different points of view about life. Each worldview is rooted in a specific emotional passion that developed as a childhood coping strategy. We are usually unaware of our ruling passion, because it operates as a blind spot, a hidden focus that affects decision making and relationships of all kinds. This book contains a short description of the types and of the ways in which each passion is acted out in one-to-one relationships, social interactions, and the arena of personal well-being that is called self-survival.

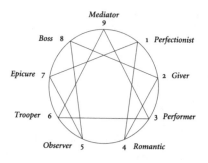

THE PASSIONS

It is the nine distinctive passions that unite the thoughts, feelings, and aspirations of each personality, usually with the effect of creating a systematic bias about life. The Pride type sees that people are in need of help. The Lust type sees the world in terms of control. The Envy type sees that something is missing, and so on through all nine types. Although they are named in the negative, the passions can also be seen as the raw material, the compost, the qualities of human nature that link each type to specific aspects of higher awareness.

I see a bit of myself in each of the nine perspectives, because they are all grounded in an appropriate emotional response. I do not have to be a Nine to merge with a loved one's agenda, nor must I be a Four to share another's pain. Each of these responses is appropriate and normal. How natural to feel afraid when we are threatened. How human to be angry when we feel misused.

THE PASSIONS AND ARROWS

The nine-pointed star, including the flow pattern of arrows, is attributed to Gurdjieff, who ascribed it to Sufi sources. The passions of sacred tradition, as described by Chaucer, Dante, and other Christian authors, were arrayed on the Gurdjieff star by Oscar Ichazo, a seminal figure in contemporary Enneagram studies.

Each type has three major aspects: the type proper, the type's reaction in times of security, and a different reaction that emerges during periods of stress or risk. The diagram's system of interlocking lines allows us to predict changing attitudes and perceptions that naturally occur when we feel secure and when we move into stress. Defenses relax during secure periods of life, such as when we have a satisfying job or a promising relationship. Risk, by contrast, implies an external stressor that creates tension. Following the flow pattern of the arrows, in risk situations you are likely to move with the arrow and adopt characteristics of the type to which the arrow points; in security you will move against the arrows, into some of the behaviors of the type in the reverse direction.

FROM VICE TO VIRTUE

Modern psychology is less than one hundred years old, but the study of type that sees the passions as a hidden feature of personality has a far longer history. In the West the passions are best known as Christianity's seven capital vices, with the addition of two generic tendencies that all types hold in common, to a total of nine (the additions are Deception [Three] and Fear [Six]). Rather than being a new psychological discovery, it would seem that our Enneagram of personality types is really a modern rediscovery of a very old concept of human development.

The Enneagram indicates that the emotional energies invested in the passions can be converted to aspects of higher consciousness. Furthermore, we are naturally motivated to transform our passion to its corresponding virtue. For example, people who feel caught in fear cannot help but value the virtue of Courage, and those who have lost their agenda (Sloth—Nine) constantly seek Right Action in life. Whether we know it or not, we seem to be set upon a path that leads from vice to the virtues of higher being.

The higher aspects of type are not merely effective psychological habits. They are ways of knowing and being that have their source in the essential, or permanent, dimensions of existence, as contrasted with the changing cycle of ordinary events. Courage, for example, emanates from essence itself, providing a source of help if we can draw on its intelligence in times of need. The qualities that emanate from essence are not the same as the clarity of mind and emotional generosity displayed by people who are psychologically mature. These gifts of the spirit belong to the realm of the divine; they cannot be grasped by analysis or recognized through our emotions because they originate in an order of consciousness beyond the limits of ordinary perception.

In linking the ruling passion of type to specific qualities of higher being, the Enneagram unites the precision of a Western clinical model with the search for existential and spiritual meaning. The Enneagram's psychological focus concerns the nine personalities and the ways in which they interact, but the power of the system lies in the links between the passions and specific aspects of higher being.

SUBTYPES

The passions can be seen as the agent of change from ordinary to higher consciousness. They are acted out through three activities that are significant enough to be called the Enneagram subtypes. These accentuated preoccupations shape the quality of our relationships and affect decisions of all kinds, often in ways that are hidden from us.

For example, the three ways that Givers (Twos) express the passion of Pride are through social *ambition,* one-to-one *seduction/aggression,* and a *privileged* attitude toward personal survival. These activities "regulate" the emotional energy of Pride and are a major factor in relating to Twos.

7

Subtype behaviors command a great deal of energy and attention, because they are expressions of the passions in the basic human experience of survival. Self-preservation concerns personal day-to-day survival, the sexual sector of life concerns survival (genetic) through time, and the social sector concerns survival in the group (herd). Whether the key behaviors assigned to each sector are actually mitigated by instinct is open to question. They may be simply type-related concerns about personal, sexual, and social survival.

SOME ENNEAGRAM HISTORY

George Ivanovich Gurdjieff (1872–1949), a spiritual teacher of enormous personal magnetism, is credited with bringing the diagram to the West. Stating that he learned the Enneagram from Sufi sources, he introduced the nine-pointed star, including the internal flow pattern that unites the points in specific ways. Living at a time when

Freud's ideas about the unconscious had yet to surface, Gurdjieff called the psychological blind spot of type "Chief Feature." The nine-pointed star diagram became the signature of his work.

Always the same motive moves Chief Feature. It tips the scales. It is like a bias in bowling, which prevents the ball going straight. Always Chief Feature makes us go off at a tangent. It arises from one or more of the seven deadly sins, but chiefly from self-love and vanity. One can discover it by becoming more conscious; and its discovery brings an increase of consciousness.[1]

Centuries ago the Italian poet Dante Alighieri described the seven areas of purgatory in practically the same language used in Enneagram studies today. Purgatory is the waiting place between earthly life and the heavenly realms, a place where sins are expiated in preparation for bliss, or permanent being. This table shows Dante's listing of the passions and their corresponding virtues from the

"Purgatorio" section of *The Divine Comedy*[2] paralleled by type descriptions produced by Oscar Ichazo, the noted contemporary Enneagram author.

TYPE	Dante (1265–1321) *The Divine Comedy, Purgatorio*		Oscar Ichazo *The Arica Training* 1970	
ONE	Anger	Meekness	Anger	Serenity
TWO	Pride	Humility	Pride	Humility
THREE			Deceit	Truthfulness
FOUR	Envy	Charity	Envy	Equanimity
FIVE	Avarice	Poverty	Avarice	Detachment
SIX			Fear	Courage
SEVEN	Gluttony	Abstinence	Gluttony	Sobriety
EIGHT	Lust	Chastity	Excess	Innocence
NINE	Sloth	Zeal	Laziness	Action

Oscar Ichazo is a contemporary spiritual teacher who provided the next piece in the Enneagram system. In a brilliant synthesis of traditional ideas, he applied Christianity's capital sins to Gurdjieff's nine-pointed star. In line with Dante's "Purgatorio," which also describes Deceit and Fear as states of consciousness, Ichazo added them to the Gurdjieff diagram, for a total of nine. Writing in 1970, Ichazo also produced the words associated with the sub-type focus of attention for each of the nine personalities.[3]

WHY STUDY TYPE?

Knowing the bias of your own type and those of the people to whom you relate improves relationships immensely. We become compassionate toward ourselves and others when we can see through the bias of our own projections. The Enneagram can put a great many human difficulties into perspective. Actions that were once interpreted as arbitrary or intentionally harmful take on a new perspective. Arbitrary behavior can be entirely logical within a given framework, and the intentions of others are often blameless once they are explained.

11

One of the Enneagram's problems is that it's very good. It is one of the few systems that concerns itself primarily with normal and high-functioning behavior rather than with pathology, and it condenses a great deal of practical wisdom into a compact system. If you can correctly type yourself and the people with whom you live or work, you have a lot of immediate information about the likely course of your relationships with these people. The good news is that we can respect each type's perspective, honoring the differences among us. The bad news is that typing easily shifts to stereotyping, where we begin to interpret one another's actions in the light of negative characteristics.

It's a small mental shift from knowing "about" type to seeing others "as" their type. When attention narrows, Eights seem controlling, Sevens seem uncommitted, and Nines seem spaced out, regardless of their actual behavior. Stereotyping causes us to interpret the behavior of others within a framework of prejudiced ideas, and at those times it seems obvious that our lives are being affected by their poor character. It helps any relationship when the partners work on both change and acceptance. We need to support one another in changing the negative tendencies of our type, but we change most effectively when we feel accepted just as we are.

One • The Perfectionist

	PERSONALITY BIAS	ESSENCE QUALITIES
HABIT OF MIND	*resentment*	*perfection*
EMOTIONAL PASSION	*anger*	*serenity*

SUBTYPE	FOCUS OF ATTENTION
ONE-TO-ONE	*jealousy*
SOCIAL	*nonadaptibility*
SELF-SURVIVAL	*anxiety (worry)*

WORLDVIEW

The world is an imperfect place. I work toward improvement.

SPIRITUAL PATH

A One's preoccupation with error points to a search for *perfection*. From a spiritual perspective, the child reacted in distress at being separated from essence. *Anger* disturbs the emotional *serenity* of being held in a perfectly balanced flow of events, while *resentment* builds from seeing the difference between life as it is and how perfect life could be. But anger can also lead to the recognition of perfection, because when anger is contained and serenity reinstated, we can learn to respond correctly at any given moment in the perfectly balanced cycle of events.

THE DILEMMA

We're all familiar with the One mind-set, because we adopt it when our values are questioned. In matters of integrity we, like Ones, search carefully for the correct approach. Once established in the right, we feel invincible. We're in service and moved by the purity of the intent; we act without concern for error.

A life dedicated to perfection requires heroic effort. Ones can't help noticing when standards slip and no one else feels guilty. How could they ignore this? Have they no shame? The tension builds. Something has to be done. If others don't notice and I do, then I'll be held responsible. A Perfectionist's conscience goes wild when errors slip by. "I saw. I knew. I'm guilty." You can't leave it alone. You feel compelled to fix it. Ones don't recognize the rising signals of their own anger; the tension feels entirely appropriate. Tension means that you're trying hard, so you brace for greater effort.

If focusing on error becomes automatic, self-observation stops. All you know is that you're working desperately hard, that you see loose ends everywhere, and you can't rest until it's finished. The scope of the task enlarges. More details surface. It's late. It's out of control. Your mind flogs you for being tired and helpless, and it's maddening that other people don't care. You don't know just how angry you are until you hear the jagged edge in your voice and feel the fury spiking through your body.

Anger leads to action. You can't hold back that bolt of lightning, and you know exactly what's wrong because it's infuriating. Something perfect has been ruined. You can't keep quiet. You're too mad to care about mistakes. Attention locks on the Right Way to fix what's wrong, and anger fuels your conviction.

Ones grow by knowing what they want instead of what would be perfect. They grow by relaxing, by letting pleasure in. You have a choice when you can read the natural signals of anger and watch your mind begin to focus on error. They are best supported by partners who can accept differences of opinion, who soften the idea that there's only One Right Way to perfection, and who bring pleasure to a relationship.

SUBTYPE FOCUS:

Anger Is Expressed Through Jealousy (Heat) in One-to-One Relationships

Perfectionists act out jealousy in an angry, possessive manner. They have such difficulty recognizing what they want, and allowing themselves to have pleasure, that any threat to gratification feels like losing a lifeline. The focal point is fidelity, but jealousy extends far beyond a sexual agreement. Ones can be jealous of people who get promoted, whose ideas are taken seriously, who are popular at work. We need to feel right. We work hard at it, and we're jealous if we're not validated. Saying "I deserve recognition" or "You should have paid attention to me" feels safer than thinking "I want" or "I need."

Anger Is Acted Out Through Nonadaptability (Rigidity) in the Social Sphere

Ones can express anger through involvement in correct causes and social ideals. Religious fervor and political conviction are prime outlets for wrath. Ones face one another across the barricades at public demonstrations, each supporting their own side as the One Right Way.

Once a position is taken, it can be difficult to absorb new information. Ones think a decision should be either right or wrong. An error blows the whole decision apart, and all the pieces will have to be reviewed again. We can't move without certainty, and in extreme rigidity, the mind closes to alternatives. We can't take in new information because it could shake the foundation of a whole belief system.

Anger Produces Anxiety (Worry) About Self-Survival

The conflict between doing what you want and doing what's right creates anxiety about survival. In this worldview, love and support are not freely given; they have to be earned by good behavior, and they will be taken away if you're "bad." To survive, you must hold onto what you have. It's a risk to be dependent. "What's yours is yours, and what's mine is mine." Everyone goes it alone in life. You support yourself and worry about being required to support others. Worry and anger go hand in hand. Repressed needs flare up and are resentfully directed at people who don't have to worry about survival.

"Why do I have to go through this?" "Why don't you have to sweat?" "Life isn't fair." A slave to circumstance.

- Notice when compulsive thinking or doing takes over. Schedule free time so that real priorities can surface.
- Question severe internal standards. Question the rules. Settle for adequacy rather than insisting on perfection.
- Avoid turning insight into self-attack, "How could I have been so wrong?"
- Get a reality check. When it seems that others are silently judging, check this out with the people involved.
- Get factual information to eliminate unnecessary worry.
- Notice when One-Right-Way thinking limits options and fair compromises.
- Learn to pay attention to the merit of other value systems.

- Focus on forgiveness: "That was then and this is now."
- Learn to request and receive pleasure.
- Question the difference between "should" statements and "want" statements.
- Use resentful feelings ("It's not fair," "They're getting away with something") as a clue to what is desirable.
- Recognize your own anger signals: putting on a happy face while feeling inwardly angry; polite words in a critically sharp voice; a smile and a rigid body.
- Weekends away. A One away from home can relax.

Two ◆ The Giver

PERSONALITY BIAS		ESSENCE QUALITIES
HABIT OF MIND	*flattery*	*will (freedom)*
EMOTIONAL PASSION	*pride*	*humility*

SUBTYPE	FOCUS OF ATTENTION
ONE-TO-ONE	*seduction/aggression*
SOCIAL	*ambition*
SELF-SURVIVAL	*me-first (privilege)*

WORLDVIEW

People depend on my help. I am needed.

SPIRITUAL PATH

From a spiritual perspective, the promptings of a higher *will* were subverted when the child turned to *flattery,* which serves the will of others. *Pride* is an inflated sense of self-worth that depends on manipulated approval, but pride is also a starting point from which to develop *humility*. When pride is converted to humility, we know our actual value to other people, and when we attune ourselves to their genuine needs, our giving can serve a higher will.

THE DILEMMA

We all enter this worldview when we see the potential in people. Their needs call forth a supportive aspect of ourselves, and we feel grateful that our efforts matter. The gifts of our own time and energy are selfless when by giving to others we take in their success as our own.

A Two's window on life looks out on other people—their wants, their potential, what they need to keep them warm. Growing up in a context where survival depended on pleasing, Twos gave to others to get their own needs met. As adults they naturally move toward people. Wanting approval, they find a way to become indispensable. Other people's needs broadcast loudly, and Twos respond by adapting. This maneuvering for position can occur without conscious awareness. Givers mold themselves to please, they are highly supportive, and they're proud to be of help.

Pride is that rush of elation we feel when someone special adores us. Twos get hooked by that kind of attention and adapt to keep it coming. If wanting to please becomes a habit, self-observation stops. You don't know that you've altered your self-presentation and forgotten your own needs. All you know is that rejection feels like annihilation, and you desperately want reassurance. Rejection is so painful that you try to get back into favor. You look for ways to fit in, you position yourself with the right people. You find that spending time with the right people is comforting. You become intrigued with their interests. You stay informed about the critical topics.

You become a good source of information and can be counted on for lively discussion. In a very short time, you're so involved that you've lost yourself by becoming indispensable.

Twos grow by discovering what they want. They grow by being alone. You have a choice when you know your real worth to others and can watch yourself enhance that worth by meeting people's needs. Twos are helped by partners who are not seduced by adaptation, who love them separately from what they give, and who see them through the crisis of having to stand alone.

SUBTYPE FOCUS:

Pride Is Acted Out Through Aggression/Seduction in One-to-One Relationships

We can become seductively attractive by adjusting our focus, taking on a partner's interests, and sharing their tastes. Twos have a talent for making people feel good about themselves and can please notoriously difficult people. In fact there's a certain pride in being the favorite, the trusted confidant, someone who can tame a tough case.

The aggressive stance entails pursuit, especially in overcoming obstacles to the relationship. Taking the active role of pursuer and the one who shoulders difficulty effectively spotlights the partner and deflects attention from ourself. Going toward people in helpful ways eliminates anxiety that we might feel rejected without these special tactics. Seduction/aggression is not a gender-specific strategy—there are seductive males and aggressive females in the one-to-one subtype.

Pride Is Dramatized Through Social Ambition

Givers maintain pride of place by ambitious social positioning: Who you know and where you're seen. Who came to your party, and were they impressed? Public image is crucial. People know you by reputation and the professional letters after your name. You attract people of stature to your circle and find yourself hosting social events.

Twos wield influence indirectly, by arranging meetings, facilitating projects, and putting people in touch who could do one another some good. Social Twos like to back a winner. Sensing the potential, they are attracted to people on the way up. Ambition is served, often unconsciously, by aligning one's own professional interests with those of a mentor, an employer, or a public figure in the field. We look out for each other. I pat your back and you pat mine. Inner-circle membership is the hallmark of ambition, and it makes Twos feel insecure to be left out. An acute awareness of shifts in allegiance and social respect develops. You protect your people by working the power structure. You want to warn them of danger and alert them to new opportunities. Twos are devotees of a loving guru, the hub of the family, and dedicated fans.

Pride Expresses Itself Through Expecting Privileged Personal Survival

Twos take pride in their own independence, believing that others depend on their help. It does not appear that the need to help arose within yourself. Feelings of selfless giving mask a need for approval and protection, but privilege is unveiled when after helping others to become successful, you are angered if returns fail to materialize. Exerting power indirectly and through other people seems more natural than working openly for your own interests. The indirect approach eases the pressure of face-to-face competition and the risk of public humiliation. If your favorite wins, you win, and in celebration of their success it's natural to expect some preferential treatment. Box seats for the inaugural.

Special attention at the victory ball. Privileged people survive well and are ushered to their proper place at the head of the line.

- Recognize your own needs rather than meeting others' needs.
- Know your actual worth to others. See the exaggeration of "being indispensable" or "everyone's best friend."
- Identify the desire to flatter and obtain approval as signs of rising anxiety.
- Observe that exaggerated emotional displays can mask real feelings.
- Notice when pride inflates and deflates. See how pride is maintained by maximizing approval and shifting blame.
- Notice when self-presentation alters to become more pleasing.
- Identify an unchanging self instead of the "many selves" that emerge to meet other people's needs.

- See through the strategy of giving to get. Learn to receive instead of overgiving.
- See when overgiving leads to exhaustion and a desire to escape.
- Discern when people really need you and when they don't.

Three ◆ The Performer

PERSONALITY BIAS		ESSENCE QUALITIES
HABIT OF MIND	*vanity*	*hope*
EMOTIONAL PASSION	*deceit*	*veracity (honesty)*

SUBTYPE FOCUS OF ATTENTION	
ONE-TO-ONE	*masculine/feminine image*
SOCIAL	*prestige*
SELF-SURVIVAL	*security*

WORLDVIEW

The world values a champion. Avoid failure at all costs.

SPIRITUAL PATH

Fixed on the idea that approval depends on image and status, Threes deceive themselves by placing *hope* in their own efforts rather than in work aligned with universal principles. In the spiritual life, hope is a felt force that guides and supports our efforts. It is an uplifting of heart that has its source in universal consciousness rather than in our own desires. Projecting an image of self-importance replaces an *honest* expression of oneself, and *vanity* exaggerates our personal merit. *Deceit* involves promoting a successful image, but when deception is converted to an honest self-expression, we may then be able to recognize the rising force of hope that originates in essence itself.

THE DILEMMA

Threes felt loved for what they achieved rather than for what they felt. Doing was valued rather than feeling. Image was valued rather than depth. As a way of flourishing in this environment, Three children learned to perform well and geared up for success. They learned to compete, to handle several jobs at once, and to promote themselves. They learned how to impress people. If the way to love is being a winner, you learn to project a winning facade.

Image can be deceptive. It's tailored to enhance results rather than to express deep needs. Self-presentation shifts in response to different occasions. You become the perfect lover, the effective professional, the leader of the pack. If your own feelings are insubstantial and unfamiliar, you can still feel good about yourself if you stand well in other people's eyes. Without the rudder of a strong emotional life to guide you, it seems natural to take your cue from other people, figure out what you're supposed to look like, and give them what they want.

When projecting an appropriate persona works, like a skilled actor you can assume the characteristics of a role. You forget that you're projecting an image. You are aware only that you hate being disliked, that heads turn when you look successful, that you can shift your self-presentation at will, and that everyone seems happier about you when you look good. If this habit becomes automatic, self-observation stops. Threes can then become victims of massive self-deception, unable to distinguish their own feelings from the feelings that come with a role.

Threes need to see through their own image. A moment of choice occurs when you can hear yourself putting a spin on your accomplishments, becoming self-promotional, or adjusting your manner to enhance the impression that you make.

Threes are helped by people who can reframe the goals of relating from surface appearances to authentic emotional depth, who are patient with a Three's habit of slipping away from feeling, and who offer loyalty to the person without buying into a convincing facade.

SUBTYPE FOCUS:

Deceit Produces an Adapted Masculine/Feminine Image in One-to-One Relationships

Threes can be masters of appearance. In intimate relationships they become the prototype of what a mate finds pleasing. In business the facade alters for maximum appeal. A top producer. Strong contenders. An attentive lover. The ideal mate. The emphasis is on form and surface. Having the right look and the best lines. The sexual subtype makes a task out of conquest. To be convincing you have to believe in yourself. You connect by projecting self-confidence. You put out hooks and see if they take. You sink the hooks that reel in approval and promote the image that falls into place.

Deceit Underlies Concerns About Social Prestige

Anonymity makes you anxious. You have to be somebody in the eyes of others or you're nobody within yourself. It hurts to see someone else hold center stage. They may be good, but you could be better. It hurts to be nobody in the crowd, so you lobby and get elected. Along the way it's natural to take on the mannerisms of a prototype. You lend yourself to the appropriate thoughts and feelings, like an actor beginning to live out a part. It makes you feel secure when heads turn toward you as a role model.

35

If you're moving between groups, you'll have different sets of clothes. It's important to look the part at the symphony or when you're driving a truck. You shoot for an image that the group values, and you know where you stand by the degree of positive response. If it's not working, you adjust, because you feel like somebody when you're appreciated.

Deceit Creates a Focus on Personal Security

Threes are preoccupied with the security that money can buy. Often rooted in the conviction that money buys safety, a survival-minded Three develops many skills to ensure job security. Even with a background of wealth, Threes have a terror of being incapacitated and unable to work. Emotional survival is attached to earnings, and a great deal of attention is paid to accumulating assets and possessions.

Your value as a person is associated with material worth, so you can deceive yourself and others about the extent of your prosperity by projecting a successful image. Happiness is often equated with affluence. Material assets will be a centerpiece of your relationship, and there is a tendency to confuse financial well-being with emotional pleasure. We'll relax after the next deal, the next promotion, the next raise in pay.

WHAT HELPS PERFORMERS

- The key word is *Stop.* Leave time for emotions to surface before hurrying to the next task. Find the fear of feelings that underlies an urgent desire for activity.
- Learn the difference between doing and feeling. Note when activity is mechanical. Robotlike work suspends feelings.
- Notice when fantasies of success replace actual abilities.
- Stay with problems rather than veering off to new projects, discrediting critics, or reframing failure into success.

- Pay attention to postponement of feelings. "I'll be happy after the next promotion," "We'll have more time after I get a raise."
- Notice when you feel like a fraud. "Nobody sees behind my mask. Only what I do is seen."
- Note unrealistic fears of failure when the work pace lessens.
- Be aware when self-reflection or support group sessions become a task to master or the next job on the schedule.
- Learn to recognize feelings. Threes may have to start by naming the sensations that underlie feelings. "My face is hot" or "My belly feels tight."
- A definite time limit for self-reflection softens the fear of emotionality. Begin with thirty-minute breaks and then back to work.
- Get support in making feeling choices rather than status choices.
- Allow people to love who you are rather than what you do.

Four ◆ The Tragic Romantic

PERSONALITY BIAS	ESSENCE QUALITIES
HABIT OF MIND *melancholy*	*original source*
EMOTIONAL PASSION *envy*	*equanimity (balance)*

SUBTYPE FOCUS OF ATTENTION	
ONE-TO-ONE	*competition*
SOCIAL	*shame*
SELF-SURVIVAL	*dauntless (reckless)*

WORLDVIEW

Something is missing. Others have it. I have been abandoned.

SPIRITUAL PATH

From a spiritual perspective, children lose awareness of their original essence when attention turns to matters of survival. Separated from that *original source* of interconnectedness with all beings, Fours became *melancholy,* or sweetly sensitive to emotional life. When *envy* strikes, emotional *equanimity* shifts to desperation, because it seems clear that others enjoy the bonding that we have been denied. A Four's insistence on authentic bonds of feeling mimics the aspect of essence in which all beings know themselves to be of one heart. But we can feel emotional union again when envious longing is brought into balance.

THE DILEMMA

We have all felt envy—that knife's twist in the heart when something precious is given to others. Fours feel deprived while others seem content. Others look satisfied with their jobs and families, while we have been denied. Fours say that it's not a matter of jealousy, that people are welcome to fulfilling pleasures; but the sight of another's happiness reminds us of what we are missing.

Envy fuels a search for the objects and status that

supposedly lead to fulfillment—money, a unique lifestyle, recognition, mates. The search is acted out by a repeating cycle of desire, acquisition, disappointment, and rejection. Romantics want the unavailable, believing that it will make them happy, and are chronically disappointed when it finally comes within reach. When a relationship that was once magnetic has passed to the stage of rejection, it begins to seem attractive again, and the cycle repeats.

If this push-pull habit of relating becomes automatic, self-observation stops. Fours don't know that they selectively see the best in what's missing. All they know is that it's unbearable to feel abandoned, that they desperately want to be reunited with a source of love, and that it's hateful to be surrounded by people who have less depth but somehow manage to be happy. If this habit of mind continues, current relationships seem pale in comparison to a distant hope. We become convinced that we've made a mistake, that happiness lies else-where, so it seems only natural to leave.

Fours grow by seeing a half-full glass rather than one that's half-empty. They grow by finding satis-faction, by knowing when they have enough. You have a choice when you can feel satisfaction and watch as the desire for something different begins to form in your mind. Romantics are helped by people who stay calm during the push-pull phase of relating, who see the good in the here and now, and who can stand fast during intense emotional tides.

SUBTYPE FOCUS:

Envy Activates Competition in One-to-One Relationships

Competition is an invigorating energy that cuts through depression and ruminating about loss. It's an "I'll show you" rush of determination that can move mountains. Competition is typically acted out in two ways: by competing for approval—"My worth goes up when I am recognized"—and through rivalry with those who receive desired attention, "My worth goes up if yours goes down." Competition easily shifts to hate, because devaluing a competitor reduces feelings of envy.

The one-to-one subtype does not usually compete with friends but can be highly adversarial to people in the same field or to a rejecting mate. They are especially vulnerable to envy if their rivals become successful or when an ex-partner enters a fulfilling new relationship.

Envy Produces Social Shame

Shame develops when we feel unworthy. We're ashamed that we don't measure up. In the social arena, envy arises when we measure ourselves against the accomplishments of others. Feelings of low self-esteem, often based on actual losses in life, perpetuate the idea that we are flawed, while others enjoy greater social respect.

There is a terror of rejection, of having that fatal flaw detected. Romantics have a desire to hide away from probing eyes, to eliminate encounters that could bring deficiency to light. They develop an unusual sensitivity to social slights and a parallel desire for recognition. It's terrible to be ignored, and worse to hear the names of the people who were invited. Image is often heightened as a protective measure. Elite memberships. A unique social presentation. Looking attractive and somewhat aloof—above the common crowd.

Envy Is Acted Out in a Dauntless (Reckless) Attitude Toward Self-Survival

Life on the edge is attractive when we feel the sadness of our condition. When we're wedged between hope and despair, why not throw caution to the wind? The dauntless character faces the fates with abandonment and a certain suicidal edge. The inner crisis generated by cycles of desire and loss infuses an ordinary event with extraordinary vitality. Life on the edge brings meaning and intensity to days that might otherwise seem mundane.

If dissatisfaction sets in when the dream is obtained, Fours have a tendency to wreck the basis of security. Money is made, lost, and made again. Lovers are seduced, rejected, and reembraced. We had to have it, we got it, we wrecked it, and now it looks tantalizing again.

WHAT HELPS ROMANTICS

- Loss is real. It needs to be properly mourned and then set aside.
- Self-absorbed sadness can be broken by physical activity and service to others.
- Eliminate self-sabotage and incompletes. Finish projects.
- See through push-pull patterns of relating. Romantics desire the unavailable and reject what's easy to obtain.

- Discover a version in oneself of what is enviable in others.
- Quiet the attraction toward dramatic acting out. Inform others about how to handle your mood swings. The steady presence of a partner softens fears of abandonment.
- Focus on the good in what's available rather than on what's missing.
- Build support systems to handle periods of sadness.
- Expect that intimacy may trigger fears of loss and abandonment.
- Recognize the sweetness of melancholy and the ability to help others in pain.

Five ♦ The Observer

PERSONALITY BIAS		ESSENCE QUALITIES
HABIT OF MIND	*stinginess*	*omniscience*
EMOTIONAL PASSION	*avarice (greed)*	*nonattachment*

SUBTYPE FOCUS OF ATTENTION	
ONE-TO-ONE	*confidence*
SOCIAL	*totems*
SELF-SURVIVAL	*castle (home)*

WORLDVIEW

The world is invasive. I need privacy to think and to refuel my energies.

SPIRITUAL PATH

Fives' preoccupation with the life of the mind mimics the pure knowing of essence. This *omniscience* is a spiritual awareness that cannot be grasped by logic or analysis, and it can be a tantalizing concept for people who are lodged in intellectualism. Spiritual knowing depends on special qualities of focus and emotional *nonattachment,* which are opposed by the contraction of *greed* and the *stinginess* that prevents Fives from sharing themselves with others. The task is to relax the retraction that separates us from our essence, so that the many aspects of spiritual knowing can emerge.

THE DILEMMA

We all adopt the Five worldview during times of scarcity. When there's not enough energy to meet our needs, we shrink our expectations. In an economy of scarcity, we learn to do with less—less involvement, fewer goods, and less emotional contact. Less produces more: more time, more energy, more personal autonomy. Less simplifies everything. Fewer desires, fewer needs, fewer rules and obligations. Freed from emotional burdens and alone with our own thoughts, Five-like, we may be nourished by the silent abundance of the mind.

An Observer's home is his castle. Low visibility, controlled contact, and uninterrupted private time. The mind becomes a good companion, an endlessly entertaining friend. The mind is also a refuge that is totally safe from invasion; we do not have to share the contents of our thoughts. Living in the mind can be remarkably self-sustaining, and observers do not feel deprived, unless desire creeps in.

There are certain physical and emotional necessities that sustain a reclusive life, and if one of these is in short supply, a tenacious desire to acquire that commodity will form. Valuing autonomy, Fives dislike having needs, and that fury feeds their desire. It becomes imperative to possess that person or those books or the treasure that has aroused their greed. Avarice is an angry need to possess, a desire so powerful that it overrides detachment. If this habit becomes automatic, self-observation stops. You dislike being forced to have feelings. You don't want needs in your life. You try to let go, but you can't. You don't have it, you must get it, and to own it you have to reach out. Caught between emotional emptiness and the fear of being engulfed by people, Fives begin to enter their feelings.

Observers develop by unifying head and heart. They grow by finding passion in life. You have a choice when you feel a spontaneous flush of emotion and can watch yourself pull back until you're empty again. They can be helped through the anxieties that attend an emotional opening by people who relate without inserting their own emotional agenda, who respect the need for time, privacy, and space, who point out overintellectualization, and who can make self-disclosure safe.

SUBTYPE FOCUS:

Avarice Is Acted Out by Protecting a Shared Confidence in One-to-One Relationships

Fives often maintain their privacy by keeping their emotional connections separated from one another. That habit lends itself to a kind of lust for intense, brief, highly meaningful encounters. Avarice in one-to-one relating refers to a preoccupation with key disclosures and emotional ties that can endure periods of separation. Confidants are the few with whom we share an "understanding." The private adviser, the personal moment, the secret love affair.

Bonds of special connection are mental treasures. They can be privately reviewed and imaginatively re-created over and over at will. They are unusually meaningful because they are few and far between and they are also securely embedded in the mind. Because Observers often experience feelings more fully when they are alone, a love enshrined in memory does not fade away.

Avarice Underlies a Preoccupation with the Totems of a Social Group

The totems of a tribe are a link between the gigantic forces of nature and the limited consciousness of humanity. They are symbols that encode a message about ancestral knowledge, and they are the focal point through which the world at large is joined with private thought.

A Five's preoccupation with mind as a source of power can develop into a passionate search for "power information." Social avarice underscores an interest in ideas and people who influence the culture. Intellectual mastery is very appealing to those who observe life; the right model properly understood provides a grasp of the true significance of events. Totem Fives are attracted to systems of study that yield big-picture accounts of social forces. Political prediction. Stock market analysis, psychoanalysis, and the Enneagram model of consciousness. It's a way to predict outer events through the command of mind. Knowledge is power, and forewarned is forearmed. Insider information is protective.

Avarice Makes a Home (Castle) the Focus for Self-Survival

Fives tend to reduce their contacts and possessions. Small luxuries can seem extravagant. These are the minimalists of the Enneagram. They take pride in doing with very little, so what they own and carry with them is going to be important. Their freedom depends on a private place in which to retire and think, surrounded by familiar belongings. The home offers sanctuary from prying eyes, draining encounters, and taxing responsibilities.

Private time and personal space can feel as vital as oxygen. Observers can be stingy with themselves, even in times of plenty. They take pleasure in abstinence, and in doing with less, because it frees them from the personal entanglements that getting more would require.

WHAT HELPS OBSERVERS

- Notice times when thoughts and emotions are withheld from others.
- Observe the hoarding of knowledge, time, energy, privacy, and personal space.
- See the control aspect of censoring information and compartmentalizing relationships.

- Observe that thinking can replace feeling and sensing information.
- Question the belief that feelings automatically lead to pain.
- Note the discrepancy between mental constructs and lived experience.
- Question the three S's: Secrecy, Superiority, and Separateness.
- Learn to value spontaneity and open-ended activity.
- See the discrepancy between feelings that emerge in privacy and the lack of feelings in face-to-face encounters.
- Question the unwillingness to display emotion.
- Find ways to be seen, to disclose, to engage rather than withdrawing.
- Realize that withdrawal forces others to become the active agent.
- Find ways to unite body and heart with mind.

Six ◆ The Trooper

PERSONALITY BIAS		ESSENCE QUALITIES
HABIT OF MIND	*cowardice (doubt)*	*faith*
EMOTIONAL PASSION	*fear*	*courage*

SUBTYPE	FOCUS OF ATTENTION
ONE-TO-ONE	*strength/beauty*
SOCIAL	*duty*
SELF-SURVIVAL	*affection (warmth)*

WORLDVIEW

The world is a threatening place. Question authority.

SPIRITUAL PATH

Six children suffered a loss of *faith* or trust in others. Contracting in *fear,* they lost contact with the power and support of essence, falling into *doubt* and the *cowardice* of worst-case thinking. However, that fall into fear initiated a lifelong preoccupation with *courage* and an inclination to search out trustworthy people and ideals. The Enneagram model of the return to essence sees the nine types as seeking those aspects of grace that relieve specific suffering. Troopers are therefore inclined, whether they know it or not, to discover faith, because they suffer from its absence.

THE DILEMMA

Fear is acted out in two ways—by fight or flight. Sixes who habitually flee (phobic) appear hesitant and want to be protected, like a man or woman who is afraid to fly. Fighting Sixes (counterphobic), who are equally afraid, would be more likely to undertake a kamikaze mission and seal themselves into the plane.

Six children know about adrenaline. They learned to be wary, to question authority, to look for veiled intentions. Skeptical and cautious, they search for hidden meaning behind a pleasant facade. Attention easily turns to worst-case-scenario thinking. An analysis paralysis: "Yes, but" and "What if?" or "Can we trust this?" Inner doubts are likely to peak when there's an opportunity to move into action. Troopers have learned that authority should not be trusted. Safety lies in predicting the motives of powerful people before risking open action.

Paradoxically, success can be frightening. Visibility equals attack. A Six looks for clues. Can you be trusted? The mind takes over: "What if?" "What if?"

If this habit becomes automatic, self-observation stops. The Trooper is primed for opposition and doubts positive support. Flooded by apprehension, thinking replaces doing. Procrastination sets in. If worst-case thinking takes over, it becomes impossible to act.

Troopers need to find trustworthy people. You have to feel safe enough to believe. You have a choice when you can differentiate between mental fears and real-life danger, when you can watch hope rise and shift to doubt. Sixes are helped by reassurance, by people who remain steadfast when the future looks doubtful, and who are faithful to their word.

Fear Underscores Strength and Beauty in One-to-One Relationships

If you're afraid of people, then caring can make you feel helpless. It can feel like falling into someone else's power. "What if they don't love me?" "What if they change their mind?" You crave reassurance, which feels humiliating. You fear abandonment, which makes you feel weak. You contract and, without realizing it, begin to doubt other people's sincerity. "They only said that to be polite," "They were being kind." It would be terrible to trust and to be betrayed. Doubting seems more realistic.

Strength and beauty are a show of power. A mask that covers inner doubt. The motive is to attract and command allegiance. A dominating beauty. The mastery of strength. The power stance is typically acted out by cultivating physical strength or beauty, maintaining a string of lovers, or displaying a dominating intellectualism. Even a frightened person can feel invincible if people think they're strong, beautiful, sexy, and smart.

Fear Is Acted Out Through Social Duty

Fears are contained by mutual obligation and commitment. The needs of the group govern behavior so we know what to expect. Self-doubt lessens when opinions are confirmed and backed by the power of collective authority. If we can't be isolated, we won't be attacked.

Duty Sixes are capable of enormous self-sacrifice for the cause, for the family, and for those islands of sanity where people are socially concerned. Political activity, self-help groups, and churches are a focus for those who find security in numbers. The compulsive variation of social commitment is played out through obligations that are spurred by guilt and fear of abandonment. Following the rules ensures your place in the group.

Affection (Warmth) from Others Lessens Self-Survival Fears

You can relax with people who know and accept you; fears disappear in the company of friends. You have a history together, you know what to expect, so you let your guard down. Sixes feel safe when someone likes them and feel endangered when people don't. There is an ongoing request for reassurance. "Do you still love me?" Distance and silence encourage doubt: "Has anything changed between us?" "What are you thinking now?" Without a reality check, Troopers fall prey to their own imagination and start to wonder, "Why didn't I get a call?" "Maybe it's off."

Given encouragement, a warm Six is devoted to friendship. When your safety is tied to other people, you want to understand them. You get close to people by disarming their anger and allying in friendship, by sticking up for them, by taking their side. Bonded by warmth, actions are motivated by friendship. We're in it together. I'm in it for you. We are not alone.

WHAT HELPS TROOPERS

- Get a reality check. Are doubts based in reality or are they imagined? Name fears out loud. Check conclusions with a trustworthy friend.
- Avoid nebulous agreements. Get clear guidelines for action.
- A support system is important for all types. For Sixes it's imperative.
- Contain procrastination by setting timelines and action checkpoints.

- Give equal time to positive options. Remember that negative possibilities seem more believable.
- Recognize times when thinking replaces action.
- Find safety in step-by-step guidelines for moving through frightening events rather than avoiding or magnifying their importance.
- Identify both fight and flight as fear reactions. Check yourself for hidden projections when others appear to be hostile.
- If attention fixates in worst-case thinking, (a) imagine best-case possibilities or (b) imaginatively exaggerate worst-case outcomes until they "overflow" by becoming ridiculous.

Seven ✦ *The Epicure*

PERSONALITY BIAS		ESSENCE QUALITIES
HABIT OF MIND	*planning*	*work*
EMOTIONAL PASSION	*gluttony*	*sobriety*

SUBTYPE FOCUS OF ATTENTION	
ONE-TO-ONE	*fascination*
SOCIAL	*social sacrifice*
SELF-SURVIVAL	*like-minded defender*

WORLDVIEW

The world is full of opportunity and options. I look forward to the future.

SPIRITUAL PATH

Work is a commonly used word that identifies the focused attention required to move beyond the personality or false-self system. If the mind becomes fascinated with the delights of outer life, then spiritual work deteriorates to pleasant *planning* and a *gluttony* for the pleasures of life. *Sobriety,* as the positive alternative to gluttony, is another word in common usage that points to a Seven's spiritual unfoldment through the route of concentration, moderation, and commitment.

THE DILEMMA

Sevens have learned to charm and disarm; they move toward pleasure and away from pain. Their escape route lies in a flow of positive options, ideas, and future visioning; when trouble hits, attention shifts and backup plans are engaged. Epicures are fascinated with high-side experience, a promising future, stimulating ideas. Committed to an active and adventurous life, these are the Enneagram's optimists. Everything's all right when you're looking ahead to a good time. Life's OK when the energy starts to run.

Gluttony is a banquet of experience. Stuffing the weekly schedule and filling the mind with plans.

Disappointments barely surface. Other options look appealing. Suddenly there's a whole new idea. Buoyed by a sense of personal worth, Sevens follow their interests, they go where they're welcomed and gravitate to people who appreciate them. Sustained by feelings of inner worth, they can move through life without much awareness of other people's pain. Life is stimulating, and each day brings its own experience; attention shifts to the next event, and life moves on.

If feelings of entitlement become automatic, self-observation stops. You don't see the positive spin on your thinking. There's a blur between potentials and fact. All you know is that being told what to do is irritating. That limitations are the product of small-minded thinking. That rules are annoying and probably unimportant—and that it feels like death when your options start to shrink.

Epicures learn by staying instead of leaving; they grow by dealing with pain. You have a choice when you've made a commitment and can watch your attention fracture. It helps to stay for one more minute instead of going away.

Sevens are helped by people who expect both pleasure and pain in relating, who value the needs and worth of a friend, who intervene when Sevens begin to slip away from commitment, and who set a framework for emotional depth.

SUBTYPE FOCUS:

Gluttony Is Acted Out Through Fascination (Suggestibility) in One-to-One Relationships

Sevens express their gluttony for stimulating one-to-one contacts in a charming manner. People are a source of endless attraction. The first sparkling hit is the best. There's a rush of initial attraction. Think where this could go. Imagine what it would be like! "This is it!"

When Sevens are fascinated by your story, they fall right into the picture. They're in your story, they're in your future, they're planning. There's click. The immediate intimacy of shared imagination makes it seem as if you're in it together. At the time, it doesn't seem like a suggestion. It sounds entirely possible. "You've been to Hawaii? I see that you loved it. Going back? It's a place I'd visit." The possibilities are fabulous. "What's your favorite place on the planet? I'd like to go there." It sounds like fact.

Epicures in long-term, monogamous relationships say that they've had to work on feeling limited by only one relationship. Commitment is the *C* word, and it's usually associated with pain. "This is it?"

Gluttony Finds Expression Through Social Sacrifice

Gluttony touches the social arena through affinity groups. Sevens like people who mirror their own sense of inner worth, who share the same philosophical ideals, and who enjoy the same activities. It feels good to be around people who like one another. The goal is to have stimulating company while pursuing the same goals that you would follow on your own.

Sacrifice Sevens see strength in numbers but are also keenly aware of the limitations that people bring to group process. It's hard not to feel martyred when people struggle and blunder. What a waste of time. You can't go solo in a group enterprise, but you wish that you could. Social Sevens are hostage to their peers because a collective effort requires personal sacrifice.

Gluttony for Like-Minded People Ensures Self-Survival

Survival Sevens can act like old-fashioned circuit riders. They visit their friends to catch up on news and see how projects are progressing. They feel secure when the different sectors of a future life plan are flourishing. The like-minded may well have been brought together through their common friendship with the Seven, who was attracted to each because of their potential contribution to a collective vision. Each defender is personally interesting to the Epicure, and each has a special quality to contribute to the whole. A gardener, a traveler, families with children, a doctor, a dancer, carpenters, a priest. Survival-minded Sevens feel reassured when they see that the different sectors of a complete life are being attended to. The conversation picks up exactly where you left off months ago, as if no time has passed. There are brainstorms, new twists of information to think about, and a gluttony for positive future visioning. Companions on the way. Like-minded defenders of the dream.

WHAT HELPS EPICURES

- Observe the attraction to stimulation and new experiences.
- Learn how opting for pleasure can also be a flight from pain.

- Note mental evasions: Multiple projects, new options, and visionary plans can herald an escape from difficulty.
- See how substituting pleasant ideas for realistic action creates procrastination and problems with completion.
- Discover how superficial activities can replace depth experience.
- Gluttony goes hand in hand with entitlement. "I deserve the best."
- Face the scope of real responsibilities and commitments.
- Note the fears that arise when self-worth is challenged. Feeling either superior or inferior to others. Wanting to stay in the superior position.
- Question the belief that opposition can be disarmed with charm.
- Notice the tendency to interpret realistic evaluation as criticism.
- Be willing to close down possibilities and commit to a single course of action.

Eight ◆ The Boss

PERSONALITY BIAS	ESSENCE QUALITIES
HABIT OF MIND *vengeance*	*truth*
EMOTIONAL PASSION *lust (excess)*	*innocence*

SUBTYPE FOCUS OF ATTENTION	
ONE-TO-ONE	*possession/surrender*
SOCIAL	*friendship*
SELF-SURVIVAL	*satisfactory survival*

WORLDVIEW

The world is an unjust place. I defend the innocent.

SPIRITUAL PATH

An Eight's preoccupation with justice points to a search for *truth*. If undivided truth prevailed, control would be unnecessary. From a spiritual perspective, children are those innocents who saw that truth could be subverted and *innocence* betrayed. Eights quickly realized that the strong dominated the weak, that vulnerability was seen as weakness, and that the good things in life went to those who could take control. The inevitable confrontation fueled *vengeance* and mobilized power, energy, and *lust* for the satisfaction of personal needs.

THE ÐILEMMA

We have all entered the Eight perspective when with complete certainty we saw the truth and acted accordingly. A force of power and fortitude wells up that cannot be compromised. The mind stops questioning. Emotions are swept away in the forward rush of action. We find ourselves in motion before we know what we will do, and we hear ourselves speak before we know what we will say. It's not a matter of courage, we couldn't draw back if we tried when the truth is at stake.

When respect is earned through power, you learn to control your feelings. You can't be vulnerable and invincible at the same time. You can't be concerned about other people's needs while they seem intent on denying needs of your own. You can't deal with tenderness or fear or regret when you're on the line of battle. The prime objective is to control the territory and to get there first.

If the top-dog approach works well, you can forget your impact on people. You are only aware of your need, and everything at your disposal will be used to achieve that objective. You forget to consult, to inform, or to get agreements, and you don't realize that you've begun to push your agenda. All you know is that you hate being deprived, that objections sound stupid and obstacles seem incidental. The energy comes on when you imagine being disadvantaged, and that rush of energy brings speed, cleverness, and strength of will. If this habit becomes automatic, self-observation stops. The results are predictable: You're the only one left on the field after the war is won.

Eights grow by questioning their ideas of justice, by hearing the other side of the story, by learning to wait. You have a choice when you can relax your own denial and watch yourself assume control by escalating the action.

Eights are helped by partners who defend their own version of the truth, who hold their ground under fire, who deal fairly, and who model the use of power in appropriate service to others.

SUBTYPE FOCUS:

Lust Underscores Possession/Surrender in One-to-One Relationships

Lust is acted out by a possessive attitude toward intimates and friends. All secrets have to be shared. Eights want to advise, to be consulted, and to take part in decisions, often taking charge of a loved one's life. Part of the pleasure of one-to-one relating involves a power struggle. It's the struggle that's interesting and, paradoxically, winning often diffuses the attraction. A battle for control infuses relationships with vital energy and is a way in which to test an associate's strength, honesty, and protective nature—all of which is fundamental to establishing commitment. Possession involves full-scale involvement in other people's lives, and when you are completely certain about their loyalty and intentions, it is finally safe to surrender control.

A Lust for Friendship in the Social Arena

Good times are magnified by good friends—those who can hold their own and assert themselves honorably. Social Eights let their feelings out within a close circle and often conduct a full-bore, ongoing quest for friendship. Their time is booked, they commandeer the volleyball court, and they have legendary stamina for carousing. There are marathon talks and deep discussions about important matters, the content of which varies from baseball to Zen, depending on your tastes.

The common factor in the lust for friendship has to do with camaraderie. You don't have to hold back because you've tested one another's limits. You and your friends look out for one another, and whatever gets said is in the spirit of friendship. You are generous with time and attention, because it's safe to kick back, say anything, open the throttle, and let the energy rise with a friend.

Lust Demands Satisfaction in the Area of Self-Survival

Survival Eights exercise territorial control over space, personal belongings, and a steady supply of creature comforts. Satisfaction depends on the simple, uncomplicated necessities of life. Just enough of everything you want is the most satisfying. The security of familiar surroundings, of knowing that your supper, your cat, and your current book are within easy reach. You can relax when you feel physically satiated.

Self-survival Eights fear being deprived, being without necessities, being out in the rain alone. They therefore develop an elaborate supply system so they'll never be in need. Food clubs, a competent laundry, a hardware store that stocks absolutely everything. It's not important to hoard, but when survival lust comes on, they know exactly where to go for ten kinds of pizza, interesting conversation, and a movie extravaganza.

WHAT HELPS A BOSS

- Allow others to initiate. Learn to wait and to listen before acting.
- Note that a desire to escalate the action, stir up controversy, or polarize a conversation may be a sign of rising insecurity.
- Identify boredom or disinterest as a possible mask for vulnerable feelings.

- Focus on the equally valid logic of other people's behavior. See the consistency within other points of view.
- See that confrontation and physical excess can cover actual feelings.
- Note that real feelings can begin with depression. Reframe "weaker" feelings as a sign of progress.
- Realize that a preoccupation with justice, protection, and control often polarizes others into being friends or foes.
- Remember to write down insights as they occur. Work against pervasive forgetting. Review insights to combat denial.
- Learn to channel anger. Both the suppression and the expression of anger can have negative consequences.
- Learn that compromise doesn't mean "quit."

Nine • The Mediator

PERSONALITY BIAS	ESSENCE QUALITIES
HABIT OF MIND *indolence (self-forgetting)*	*love*
EMOTIONAL PASSION *sloth (laziness)*	*right action*

SUBTYPE FOCUS OF ATTENTION	
ONE-TO-ONE	*union*
SOCIAL	*participation*
SELF-SURVIVAL	*appetite*

WORLDVIEW

My efforts won't matter. Don't make waves. Keep the peace.

SPIRITUAL PATH

Babies "are" essence, in that their awareness is permeated by the unconditional *love* of pure being. But as personality formed in early life, we became *indolent,* or forgetful about our spiritual nature. *Sloth* is an overaccommodation, a desire to live comfortably and mechanically rather than initiating *right action* toward those aspects of life that support spiritual renewal. Nines avoid conflict and merge with the agendas of others, which mimics the quality of love that unites all beings.

THE DILEMMA

We all enter the Nine perspective when we feel inseparable from others. Boundaries go down when someone else's life becomes the motive for our own. Once merged, it feels like one skin and a single being. There's energy for a partner's agenda. Their interests feel vital, their opinions seem valid. There's enthusiasm for their life, which has become the focus of our own.

A tension develops between wanting to comply so as to be loved and wanting to defy, to assert your independence. The quandary is, "Do I agree and go along?" or "Do I disagree and create conflict?" Agreement feels like giving in, but it's hard to say no. Once you're merged with someone else's life, choice no longer matters. You can see the worth of their position more easily than your own.

Sloth means being lazy about life. Decisions are difficult when conflicting opinions appear to have equal merit. Attention cycles from central issues to secondary matters. You get sidetracked to chores and backlogs of unfinished business. Your momentum slows, and without your realizing it, a holding pattern develops. Energy for primary goals gets siphoned off to secondary activities.

Nines develop by paying attention, by structuring their own agenda, by staying on track. You have a choice when you can watch yourself absorbing a new position. You can learn to separate and pay attention to yourself. Nines are helped by partners who encourage separate goals, who provide solid reinforcement for progress, and who remind Nines of those deeply held purposes that depend on personal choice.

Laziness Underlies a Search for One-to-One Union

Forgetful of their own direction, Nines often need others to focus effort and provide a reason for being. Nines can be swept along by other people's enthusiasm, developing a sense of mutual existence at the expense of maintaining their own individuality. Union provides focus and energy; feelings of being overlooked will vanish in a psychologically undivided state. Nines adopt other people's positions by thinking in the way that a partner thinks and taking on other people's feelings. There are mergings of identity. Moments of "weness." We are the same being. "Who has this face?"

Laziness Is Acted Out Through Social Participation

Participating in group activities can be a comforting way to feel included and loved. It can also be the place of greatest laziness for social Nines, because the energy that could be spent in meeting personal agendas is instead shunted to activities.

Group goals, procedures, and an ongoing time-table demand predictable expenditures of energy. Groups also allow members either to participate minimally or to take responsibility and leadership when they have energy to burn. Social Nines are inclined to join and to attend on a regular basis without making a full inner commitment. The question stays open. "Do I agree or disagree?" "Do I belong here or not?" "Do I like this or not?" Ambivalence is familiar.

Laziness Creates Appetites in the Area of Self-Survival

All Nines have a tendency to replace essential goals with inessential substitutes, but appetite Nines can develop a voracious attachment to the replacement. Small pleasures are an automatic source of comfort and a temporary replacement for love.

There's immediate relief in zoning out on food or mystery novels. There's the familiar solace of sitting and watching TV. Security-minded Nines don't realize that they're shelving a personal agenda when they're gripped by appetites, such as shopping fever. The rising interest in indulging an appetite doesn't feel at all lazy. It feels exhilarating.

WHAT HELPS MEDIATORS

- Notice when others become the referent for action. "Do I agree or disagree with them?" "Do I go along with them or not?"
- Use deadlines, structure, and positive feedback to support personal goals.
- Learn to shift attention when obsessive thought about the pros and cons of a decision take over.
- Focus on feelings when obsessive thinking begins. Ask, "What do I want?" instead of "What do others want?"
- Learn to recognize the signals of passive aggression. Nines control by slowing down and refusing to act. Recognize this passivity as anger.

- See anger as good news in disguise. Anger can reveal a previously submerged position.
- Nines decide more easily when they're given choices. They know what they don't want more readily than what they do want.
- Find the feelings that are numbed by inessentials such as TV, errands, and other ways of postponing action.

Epilogue

When an ancient teaching reappears, we might easily assume that it has been transposed as an intact transmission from the past. Nothing could be further from the truth. The Enneagram is one of the jewels of sacred tradition that is currently being reset in a contemporary context of psychological and spiritual ideas.

This is a living tradition, in the sense that it lives in the self-observations of the people who inhabit the types. Those who embody the nine passions speak as living authorities about their own thoughts and feelings, showing us the logic of different points of view.

It is a system that is crucial for our time because it promises to unite the private work of psychological insight with the goals of spiritual realization.

Endnotes

1. C. S. Nott, *Journey Through This World: The Second Journey of a Pupil* (New York: Samuel Wiser, 1969), 87. It is useful to note Nott's choice of the word *vanity* as a generic source of personality bias in conjunction with the seven capital sins. Vanity was placed as the cognitive (mental) aspect of the deceit passion by Oscar Ichazo at the Three point of the diagram. Ichazo also placed the generic characteristic of Fear at the Six point, to a total of nine capital tendencies.

2. Paolo Milano, ed., *The Portable Dante* (New York: Viking, 1947), "Purgatorio" section.

3. Robert Frager, ed., *Who Am I? Personality Types for Self-Discovery* (New York: G. P. Putnam's Sons, 1994), 221–29.

About the Author

Helen Palmer is the primary source for Enneagram Studies in the Oral Tradition, a teaching method that unites psychological integration with the goals of sacred tradition. Her work includes organizational consulting services, a full Enneagram professional training program, and a bicoastal school for spiritual studies. A current international teaching schedule is available from her office, as are referrals to graduates of the Enneagram Professional Training who work in your area.

A video series, *Nine Points of View,* and a listing of audio cassettes are available on request. To receive further information, please contact:

Workshops in the Oral Tradition with Helen Palmer
1442A Walnut Street
Berkeley, California 94709
Voice (510) 843-7621
Fax (510) 540-7626